WEDDINGS
A | TIPICA

Madrid, 2017

EDICIONES EL VISO

The **A-tipica** team has had a wonderful time preparing this book. This has been the feeling in each of the projects developed throughout our company's fifteen years of history, and this is thanks to our team, part of the A-tipica family, and without whose collaboration none of this would have been possible: Paloma and Marta, who personify infinite creativity and integrate the art department, where they shape our ideas; to Moira, who, together with Paola and Claudia, supervise projects from start to end; to Yolanda and her efficiency without limits; Terry, who, from the office with Marina, takes care of the company's communications and shares all the fantastic pictures posted about our work; Alberto and Renata, the production department, creators of wonders at the A-tipica warehouse; and Barbara, whose administrative work makes everything run smoothly within the company.

In addition, we can't forget our suppliers; without them our tale could not be told. Side by side we form a team that works to make everything run to perfection. For this reason, we are especially grateful to florists, tent assemblers, carpenters, upholsterers, lighting and sound companies, support and logistics people, transportation and catering services, restroom staff, photographers, printers, musicians, artists and so many others who have helped us to grow over the years, being part of A-tipica in every event and making our designs materialize. We thank you all from the bottom of our heart.

AN ATYPICAL
STORY

Cristina Ruiz Montesinos

In the spring of 2002 Cristina Soriano made a decision that would change her life completely, as it would also change the national scenario of weddings as an act of social importance. Raised in the Philippines, where celebration is an essential part or their culture, this tenacious businesswoman undertook the task of helping to organize her daughter Paola's wedding. A small pink notebook was her first companion in a one-way journey which she could have never guessed would be so complex. Juggling with caterers and there being no companies providing a comprehensive service covering all wedding needs, Cristina, with a passion for decoration and being a splendid hostess, was forced to become the wedding planner for her own daughter. All decisions would contribute to making such a crucial moment an unforgettable memory. And fifteen years later, what had emerged as a family challenge became a story worth telling.

With her imprint on every detail and boosted by her excitement, the process initiated by Cristina culminated with what today is known in Spain as A-tipica. A temple in the world of event planning and a safe gamble in the wedding business where, for thirty years, each one of her daughters have battled with determination and charisma. Andrea, Paola, Carla and Marina lived that first adventure together and have since become increasingly inspired by the project, contributing to its colossal success at different times in their lives.

Claudia Aguirre

Paola Herrera

Convinced that a wedding should be something more than a mere incidental family get-together, Cristina first teamed up with Andrea, her eldest daughter, and with one of her school friends, Alejandra, to launch the first A-tipica store in a basement just down the road from Madrid's National Auditorium. Paola joined in 2005, the year Andrea decided to leave Madrid, and two years later Claudia joined them as a partner, substituting Alejandra. Carla, the third sister, joined a little later taking care of press and communication, and, when the company had already reached cruising speed, Marina — the youngest — who had been collaborating every summer in her teens, joined full-time to launch the lifestyle area.

Today, that tiny showroom has turned into a bright space in Madrid's Plaza de la Villa de Paris, where A-tipica divides its projects into three areas that define its business, that is, decoration, weddings and event planning. The matriarch, although no longer corporately involved in the project, remains on the alert, and her daughters Paola and Marina as well as Claudia, now in charge, often seek her advice. After all it was she who, with her good taste and innate elegance, organized the best parties and dinners ever remembered in the family clan.

THE A-TIPICA STYLE

Both the wedding scenario and the perception that exists around the wedding planner concept have changed drastically in the last fifteen years. As Paola says: "When we started, in 2002, we had to justify our business with tooth and nail, defending our professionalism and convincing people that this is not an extraordinary expense but a necessary one". At the beginning, people didn't believe much in detail, yet this team stubbornly defended the importance of each and every detail as a crucial value.

With unusual charisma, A-tipica can take all the merit as the first to establish details, now common in weddings, such as the table name cards in watercolors, oriental-style fans — the result of inspiring travels — the still lifes of flowers or the delicate lettering of all the texts from invitations to final menus.

Marina Herrera

Years of work that sum up its highly personal style and match the excitement of each couple entrusting A-tipica with their wedding. A-tipica's first slogan, "Down to the last detail," responded to a historical moment in which *ad hoc* craft and luxury were notably lacking in most events, so often focusing on menu and drinks only. Now that times have transformed and boosted desires, the slogan is "We are your ally", in becoming a key partner for the fair budget distribution in each event.

These two slogans give rise to the idea of providing comprehensive advice. That is, to enjoy the preparation of the most special day of your life knowing that any hitches are addressed even before they appear. In the event of rain, A-tipica has the infrastructure to protect the guests against the weather. If the bride and groom are not into conventional entertainment at the wedding party, A-tipica will move mountains to hire a singer or international music band to offer a unique performance. Their success at doing magic to make the wildest dreams come true is such that their impact has reached countries like France, Italy, the United States or the Philippines. "At each venue, you need to work with an absolutely unique *modus operandi*, because, even though promotion is achieved through word of mouth, at every wedding you have to work as if it were the last", argues Paola. If it goes well, perhaps half the guests will speak wonders about you. "But if you make a slip, absolutely all of the wedding guests will give you a bad report".

The amazing portfolio behind them is full of all types of brides. This is due to their versatility and an innate power to adapt to each client without any prejudices, while keeping up the creativity. Good taste doesn't make you better or worse: bringing dreams together is what generates, in short, the perfection of the results.

AN EXPANDING UNIVERSE

For Marina, Claudia and Paola, the world of wedding planning has entirely become an art that neither can nor should decline, so they intend to expand it and nourish it with trends and novelties. They can be seen doing a TV program on the Canal Decasa channel or giving a masterclass on Condé Nast College, not a question of ego but because they believe in creating a scenario that favors fair competition, that dignifies and promotes wedding planners and defends them, in short, as a professional and responsible figure.

Based on that belief, the circle of collaborators around them grow to trust them, caring and praising each other whenever they can. Florists, light technicians, musicians, assemblers, assistants, caterers, small hands that work the magic and achieve the feat of making a dream come true, the dreams of those who hire them.

Much more than a family. From left to right all the members of A-tipica: Andrea and Carla Herrera, their mother Cristina, Paola and Marina Herrera and Claudia Aguirre.

"It is the bride and groom who dictate the initial inspiration: the venue, their personalities and their tastes in terms of travel, films, literature or music. Each one of those details concoct the final magic", they admit. In this matter, the only limit is the sky: they are able to listen and do crazy things like getting the tents of an event shipped by air from Belgium, setting up a stage for a band from Monaco or starting to landscape a house ten months before the appointment so that it looks its best on the special day. All this with an intimate satisfaction that they readily admit: "Getting a thank-you note the day after the wedding, when you're exhausted after working as hard as you can, is probably the best part of our work. When you find that all that human investment, which is not achieved by working for companies, bears fruit, then you are close to believing that you've done the right thing".

THE FUTURE

A-tipica's universe is in constant change since its creation, but it's in 2008 when a step forward gains relevance. That summer, Marina, the youngest of the sisters, presented as her thesis at Emerson College in Boston a project entitled "A-Ti-pica Living". An initiative that raises the furthering of the company's proposals beyond the appointed event day, offering furniture and decoration, from artisan candles to specialized workshops. Far from remaining a mere academic essay, this new department has joined the family and is a temple of infinite alternatives as to what, how, when and where for a dinner, christening, lunch or occasion for remembrance. In 2013 they expanded this peculiar showroom, which became a physical store on the Madrid Street of General Castaños and an online shop where you can find interiors and lifestyle items, usually the result of the trips that nourish their inexhaustible curiosity.

With respect to the new generations, who have replaced routine agendas with cutting-edge technology and who live subjected to the saturation and over information of social networks, the game has changed: everything is urgent, and the worst competition for any company is Google's ferocious search engine. And A-tipica has a clear goal even for this challenge: to become that catalyst filter capable of helping every couple to bring their wedding as close to what they always dreamed as possible. This book, without a doubt, will be a good example of it and, at the same time, a generous reminder of A-tipica's legacy also summed up as a hopeful look to the future.

17

TO ROME WITH LOVE

Francesca, Italian, and Jaime, Spanish, met working as a stewardess and pilot respectively. When they decided to marry, they chose Rome, dazzled by the Odescalchi Castle, a wonderful medieval monument perfect for bringing the two families together on such an important day. They decided to hire A-tipica to plan a wedding in which the Spanish and Italian cultures should be present in every detail.

The A-tipica team traveled there to meet all the suppliers confirming that the venue was spectacular. The best catering company in Turin was hired, renowned for their impeccable presentation. The logistics related to all the guests was specially focused on, as they would be coming from all over the world.

In terms of the decoration, A-tipica followed the bride's preferences: avoiding cut flowers and an excess of color, and rather opting for the range of greens. Therefore, lush and tall *ficus* trees were installed in the church, and the aisle was filled with candelabra enhancing the grandeur of the Castle. Lighting was a priority to tone down any solemnity: White *Freesia* was placed on the dinner tables to give some light, in centerpieces mounted on tall candelabras. The tables, to live up to their surroundings, were laid with tableware chosen for the occasion, with hand-cut glasses, and every detail was chosen very carefully. Airplanes, so important in the couple's life, featured the place cards designed by A-tipica.

To end the dinner, in the next-door living room, a spectacular buffet of desserts was displayed at different levels. Then the nightclub, where the lighting and the trees—the bar was all covered with natural green leaves—emulated a forest. A wedding undeniably marked by a medieval romanticism from start to end.

To avoid distracting attention from the charm of the castle, a prop company was hired to decorate the whole interior.

All the castle exteriors and the cloister were decorated with over three thousand candles.

The bridal bouquet was very delicate
and fresh, made with green leaves and
white flowers

The church was filled with lush *Ficus*.
The guests followed the ceremony aided
by mass books prepared in two languages.

The flowers in the dining hall were placed on tall candelabras seeking certain warmth in the lighting.

The table was meticulously prepared with every detail, laid with varying models of cut-glass glassware and customized menus, and name cards in watercolors made especially for the occasion.

Castello di Bracciano, 3 Maggio 2014

Plin alle zucchine,
fiori di zucca e leggera fonduta di Parmigiano

Filetto di Fassone in crosta di sale con intingolo di erbe

Torta Nuziale

Buffet di dolci

Castell de Raimat Chardonnay 2013
Viña Pomal Centenario Reserva 2009

Airbus 320

In the living room adjacent to the dining area a spectacular buffet of desserts was displayed, placed at different levels, with a selection of candies prepared by a catering company from Turin.

The bride and groom gave their guests a classic Italian gift, "confeti", which are sugar-coated candies. They were presented in a container specially chosen by the bride called "bomboniera".

The cocktail bar was covered with natural green leaves to simulate the effect of a forest. The lighting in different reddish and blue colors was key to recreate an atmosphere of mystery and fun.

The catering company prepared a very original dinner with different types of pizzas that were prepared on the spot in an oven adjoining the halls.

WELCOME TO MIAMI

When Diana and Diego came to A-tipica, they had a clear idea about three things: they wanted to celebrate a wedding in Miami—their place of residence— it should feature the bride's bohemian lifestyle, yet keeping to the traditions, and they needed help. Based on this and after travelling to the United States to conduct research, the A-tipica team, helped by a local wedding planner, decided that the ceremony would be held in a church near the beach and, later, all the guests would move to the Miami Seaquarium, where a sit-down dinner would be served. At this point the first difficulty arose: The Seaquarium is not a place usually hosting weddings and protection of the animals is their priority, so A-tipica had to adapt to this situation.

The space finally chosen to erect the tent, after a week for assembly, was a nice grassy area with spectacular views of the Miami skyline because, without a doubt, the city was to be the main thread of the whole wedding. The skyscrapers witnessed an event fraught with vintage details, in honor of the bride, carefully chosen decor and an unforgettable party. The space was enhanced with a mixture of undressed tables, which meant that the tableware, as well as the floral decoration, would take center stage.

As would the music, since the bride's father is a musician. The bride and groom chose all the church choir pieces and the repertoire of a live band. All the tables were labeled with names of indie music festivals and all the guests ended up dancing, dressed up with costume accessories, to the rhythm of the DJ. Fireworks were the final touch for a perfect Miami Beach-style wedding.

CONGRATULATIONS DIANA & DIEGO ON YOUR WEDDING DAY !

The spirit of the city of Miami marked the relaxed and cheerful atmosphere of the wedding. During the pre-dinner drink, a plane with a banner surprised the bride and groom, congratulating them.

To give the wedding an atmosphere with a rustic and somewhat hippie touch, extreme care was taken to choose the decor featuring natural wood and combining different chairs. The tables were named after festivals as a gesture to the day that the couple met, precisely in Coachella.

The flowers were one of the bride's priorities. She wanted them to be colorful, with touches of orange and plenty of daisies, her favorite flower. Combined, two-level centerpieces balanced the scene.

The wedding venue was unique
with spectacular views of the Miami
skyline.

The tent was a circus model,
large and high, making everything
come together in a single space.

Fireworks with the spectacular
Miami backdrop wrapped up
a memorable party.

A PICNIC IN THE GARDEN

Since Ivo and Carolina decided to celebrate their wedding at the groom's parents' home in Madrid, they thought it was essential to be helped by wedding planners such as A-tipica to get the best out of the house and put forward an original idea, out of the ordinary. They kept in mind at all times that the celebration would be different and fun.

For the civil ceremony, a glass walkway was placed across the pool that the couple crossed to reach a spectacular ceremony table with flowers in shades of blue, purple and green.

The great surprise of the wedding was that, evoking an open-air party, the dinner was available on various food stands. They were white, of braided wood, with beige awnings, with different food and the guests could rise from their long tables, dressed with black-checkered tablecloths, to choose and serve themselves from each stand: at the time, still not a very widespread idea that served as a precedent. The guests found at their tables a booklet with an explanation about the different stands and, to the rhythm of a Cuban band, the dinner progressed with swing.

The flowers of the tables were tailored to the carefree atmosphere of the event, choosing aromatic plants presented in zinc cans or wicker baskets filled with flowers.

Fireworks and Chinese lanterns launched by the guests were the perfect way to wrap up this romantic and fun garden party.

Ivo and Carolina had A-tipica's
help to transform the garden of the
groom's family home into a dream-
like setting for their wedding.

A glass walkway was placed over the pool leading to the ceremony table, decorated with flowers in blue, purple and green, where the bride and groom took their vows. The guests followed the ceremony. The mass books were fan-shaped, fulfilling a double function.

Clearly inspired in the countryside, a large garden space was available to install long tables dressed with custom-made black and white checkered tablecloths. Black folding rustic chairs and aromatic flowers completed this sophisticated picnic.

The menu, designed by Artepapel, was presented in a small hardcover book covered in gray fabric, a gesture to the groom's mother, an editor. Inside, the guests read about all the dishes at the different stands surrounding the tables.

Bouquets of natural flowers were placed as if they had just been picked from the field. The cocktail bars were laid with flower centerpieces with limes and lemons.

Evoking a sophisticated open-air party, the dinner was available at various food stands assembled for the wedding. They were white, of braided wood, with beige awnings and featuring various types of food so that the guests could choose.

A FOREST OF PANICULATA

A Lebanese couple wanted to get married in Barcelona fleeing the traditional wedding format typical in their country—more overelaborate and crowded—and organize a smaller and more familiar event.

They wanted their wedding to have an informal, rustic air, where entertainment was paramount, and the Ribas country manor—one of the options shuffled—was the perfect place.

On a green esplanade the ceremony was prepared with simple white chairs and decorated with paniculata. The bridesmaids threw petals and carried a banner with the legend "Here comes the Bride", in an emotional ceremony. Then a snack was served with a fresh and Mediterranean-flavored menu.

When the guests went round to the back of the garden they found a magical spot: a sky of light bulbs, with lanterns suspended above chill out areas, which illuminated long natural wooden tables. Tall paniculata centerpieces were arranged on a base of white flowers and greenery.

It was a dinner alive with movement, with buffets on food stalls and live piano bar music. Instead of cake, a giant piñata surprised the guests and, upon its arrival, everyone lit up their table sparklers showing that magic is real.

The Ribas country manor was the venue
chosen for the celebration, both for the
civil ceremony and dinner and dance that
followed. The ceremony took place in the
gardens, in front of the house, decorated
with white folding chairs and numerous
white paniculata centerpieces.

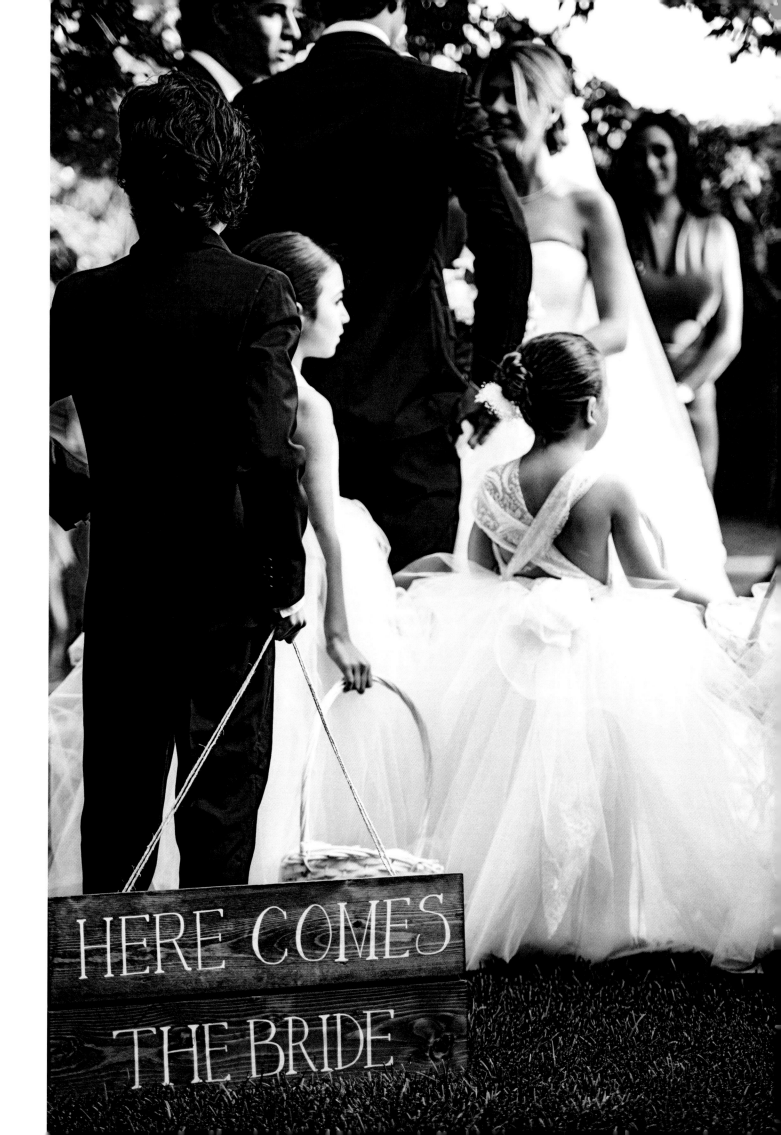

According to Lebanese tradition,
the guests dance throughout the
wedding, from the very start. That's
why, in the center of the dining area,
there was the dance-floor, cheered
with live piano bar music.

The catering company service prepared samples of fresh and simple dishes such as gazpacho or crudités with garden vegetables, so that the guests, most of them foreign, could taste the typical regional dishes.

The lighting and table layout were designed to enhance the beauty of the manor's back garden. Light bulbs and hanging lanterns over the guests created a magical effect.

White shabby chic platters were set on the tables with a white basket of bread, which added a rustic touch to the decor. At each place, the guests found a thank-you note from the bride and groom. They also designed a wedding logo in the bride's home country, embossed on all the wedding cards.

Barcelona / us, our true love, and the people we love most / June 1st 2014 /

Lara & Ralph

The furniture featured textiles with floral motifs, along with wrought iron lamps and bouquets, creating beautiful still lifes spotted around the garden.

Each catering stand had its own lighting and decoration, so guests toured the magical market tasting the best dishes prepared for the occasion.

The party followed inside the manor under illuminated vaulted ceilings. Disco mirror balls and shelves filled with candles witnessed a party where a famous DJ from Beirut left the guests breathless. The entertainment was the key to the night's success.

AN ENGLISH GARDEN IN BILBAO

When they came to A-tipica María and Dani had already decided where they would celebrate their wedding. It would be in the Caserío of Olagorta, a typical Basque farmhouse with lots of charm near Neguri. They had also decided on the date: July 25th. Having pretty clear ideas of what they liked and what they didn't like, they collaborated enormously to create the perfect project. The big challenge was to prepare everything so that the weather in Bilbao, often rainy, wouldn't catch them by surprise.

The bride adored flowers. She had taken several flower-related courses in London and the flowers were her highest priority. We thus decided to create an indoor garden inside the house using a range of soft colors and with the typically wild and rambling design of an English garden. So the result was something beautiful, lucid and also youthful and cheerful, as it was to be a daytime wedding in the countryside for a young couple.

Guests were greeted upon their arrival with a saxophonist's music who played as he walked among the people, creating a cheery atmosphere. An original touch was provided by a giant ice sculpture that served as cooler for the champagne bottles and prettily decorated the cocktail area. As there were many wedding guests, the luncheon took place inside the house and in an adjoining building. A transparent hexagonal tent in white and green fabrics was erected to accommodate the guests on a day throughout which the rain did not make an appearance.

The arrival of the groom in a classic convertible car was one of the many nice touches given to María and Dani's wedding.

The ceremony was held in the Church of Nuestra Señora del Carmen, in Neguri. As it is small and quite dark, flowers were used in greens and whites to lighten the shadows.

Flowers were everywhere to
recreate a garden inside the house:
climbing the stairs, creeping up the
columns and even along the beams.
Everything was covered in flowers
materializing the bride's dream.

Nice touches were planned to make a difference, such as the cocktail bars, decorated with rust-like wallpaper, or a giant ice sculpture that served as cooler for the champagne bottles.

The bride's bouquet was a tightly assembled ball of white carnations.

After lunch, the guests emerged from the tent to find a small stage where a music band cheered the first phase of the party.

At dusk, a DJ kept the party going until well into the night.

THE GREAT CIRCUS

On July 14th, 2012, the circus wedding (as it is remembered by in A-tipica) in León was a real challenge. The couple, María and Uri, owners of the creative agency Calera Studio, designed the invitations, menus and stationery, but also had a clear idea about this day: to start with the civil ceremony at home leading, very subtly and throughout the day, to a real circus inspired by those typical of the early twentieth century. At the house entrance, origami birds, symbolizing friendship, and colorful circus strips adorned the arrival to the sound of the music played by the Desvariétés band, also in charge of cabaret and cuplé performances in the hours that followed.

Under a white marquee flanked by turquoise poles with tiny red stars, which were reminiscent of circus decor, the lunch was served while the guests hardly sensed the surrounding metamorphosis. Between events, they could rest in the gardens and in the swimming pool (they were given swimming gear commensurate with the epoch of inspiration), until a master of ceremonies invited them to witness the show in an improvised drama theater.

After the performances, the dinner, served on standard, long wooden tables in the open air, served as an interval to make the third transformation possible: a huge disco where the music continued until daybreak.

The wedding was held at the bride's house in León. The civil ceremony took place at the front main entrance of the house decorated for the occasion. Ribbons hung from the guests' chairs in colors also used on the invitations, and which repeatedly featured the day's events.

Origami birds, according to a legend, make all wishes come true. That's why they were placed over the bride and groom and the officiator, hanging from a transparent surface to simulate their flight over the ceremony.

The tables, where lunch was served, were rectangular and differed from one another, and displayed large red numbers. The flowers, of many colors and kinds, created a beautiful show.

The bride painted little animal figures in white that were placed next to the centerpieces, and each guest was given a jar of jam.

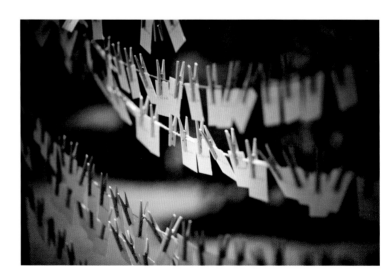

Elisabeth Blumen decorated small
resting spots under garden tents.

Original forms of entertainment were available to the guests, such as a table soccer, board games or old-fashioned swimsuits for the pool.

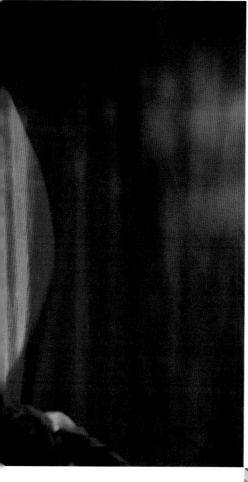

A master of ceremonies handed out tickets allowing entrance to the tent to enjoy the show. There the audience discovered a theater setting with a stage under the heading "MU Circus", referring to the names of the bride and groom, María and Uri, and a large star on the floor.

Once the performances were over, the guests enjoyed the dinner, presented in stalls decorated with the same circus motifs used in the entire wedding and supplied with carnival style food: Burgers, ice cream and some with a Spanish touch such as Galician octopus and grilled meat. All under a canopy of light bulbs.

THE CRYSTAL PALACE

Preparing the venue for a celebration is an event planner's obligation, but A-tipica went a step further in this wedding because, as it was taking place on the family estate, a landscaping project was organized months earlier to prepare the garden areas for the event. Grass and plant seeds were sown so ensure that everything would be just perfect for June 22nd, the date chosen by Nicole and Javier.

The bride wanted a romantic wedding with a dramatic touch. But, in addition, entertainment should be an essential part. Romantic, pretty, but most of all fun!

For the ceremony, the bride dreamed of a forest that was recreated by flowery trees to give shade and attempting a similar effect with a mural painting of a forest. A painting of the Virgin was hired from an antique shop and we created a background of plants to make it the most important spot of the religious celebration. A gospel group provided an emotional touch.

Once the ceremony was over, the appetizers were served at a variety of stalls and Elton John Glam rock style music was played on a grand piano. At dinner time, grass-covered doors were opened leading to a green iron and glass marquee that looked just like a greenhouse, with chandeliers hanging from the ceiling inside cages for the desired dramatic touch. The centerpieces brimmed with pastel colored flowers and peaches.

A London music band kicked off the party. This was followed by a DJ along with live sound keeping the party going until dawn, when even a violinist appeared with the fireworks. The fun was guaranteed!

  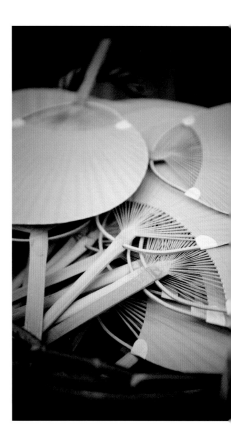

The ceremony was held outdoors and, with the help of green oriental-style fans and white parasols, guests attempted to avoid the heat.

The mass books featured the same watercolor as the painting presiding over the ceremony. The witnesses' names were handwritten at their tables.

It was important for the religious ceremony to reflect respectful solemnity, even though it was being held outdoors. For that reason, a very large picture of the Virgin was hired to preside the event.

In addition, shade was provided by trees with white blossom recreating a forest.

Once the ceremony was over cocktails were served from a variety of stalls with flavored water to greet the guests.

At dinner time, grass-covered doors opened leading to a green iron and glass marquee, like a greenhouse. Chandeliers inside cages hung from the ceiling and provided the dramatic touch so desired by the bride.

The centerpieces brimmed with pastel-colored flowers mixed with fruit.

Some large pots with hydrangeas skirted the marquee, so that no corner went unnoticed.

Entertainment was an essential part of this wedding. A London music band kicked off the party. The disco floor was transparent and the lighting came from some spotlights at the bottom of the pool.

A DJ, aided by live instruments and singing, kept the party going until dawn. The final surprise was a violinist who arrived with the fireworks, the fun was guaranteed!

A SUMMER NIGHT'S DREAM

The protagonists of this wedding were a very young couple, who came to A-tipica full of enthusiasm. They were sure that they wanted to marry in a private house, with a very romantic tent and taking advantage of the garden hedges full of jasmine in bloom.

Everything was inspired by *A Summer Night's Dream*. The intention was that, although the guests were in a tent—something necessary in the north of Spain—they would feel like they were in a secret garden. To do this, a round tent was erected with walls of jasmine and mirrors. Within this area, music, fun and fireworks made a magical wedding.

The church interior was decorated with daffodils, just like the bride's bouquet. When they left the church, they were greeted with a typical regional pasiego dance, accompanying the guests to the cocktail area decorated with large pots of plants and flowers, seating areas and traditional food. When the cocktail ended, there was a little rain and the guests went inside the tent, which resembled a dream.

The dance floor in the center of the tent was a shiny surface that mimicked water and in the middle, there was a Saint Honoré dessert. The top cover was of green and white pleated fabric and in its central area there was a huge LED screen simulating a starry night.

The dinner was romantic and magic, and when the dessert arrived, the guests went out to contemplate the fireworks. Back inside the starry sky became a giant screen that projected different geometric figures achieving the goal: the evening was a dream.

The bride's bouquet, daffodils, matched the church decoration that also displayed the same flowers.

Coming out of the church, they were greeted with a typical regional pasiego dance. The dancers led all the guests with music and dance from the church to the cocktail area.

The cocktail area had the same floral
decoration as outside the church, with
large pots of plants and flowers in cheerful
and eye-catching colors such as red and
pink. Then, when going in to dinner,
everything became green and white.

In the north of Spain you always
need to have your umbrella ready.
At the end of the cocktail, it began
to rain and white umbrellas were
provided to all the guests so that
they could take cover moving to the
dining area.

Each guest received a ceramic bowl, made especially for the wedding, with almonds that the groom's mother brought from Greece according to the tradition of their country.

Guests enter the tent as if going into a secret garden. The tent fabrics and the LED ceiling emulating a starry sky produced a magical atmosphere.

With the latent inspiration of *A Summer Night's Dream*, it was intended that the guests, even though they were inside a tent—something necessary in the north of Spain— would feel like they were in a secret garden. They entered through curtains adorned with garlands of magnolia.

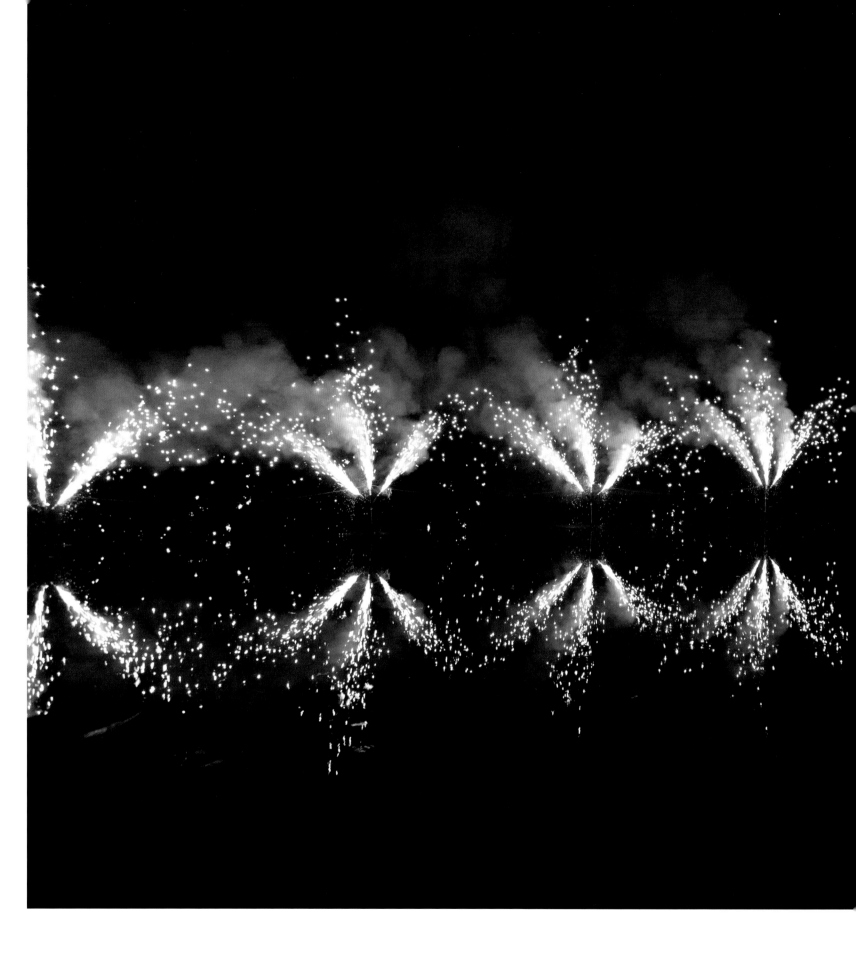

After the dessert, the guests came
out of the tent to contemplate
the fireworks.

THE TASTE OF MAJORCA

The bride was a Martha Stewart collaborator and she had two obsessions for her wedding day: The table setting and the invitations. Although the couple live in New York, they chose Majorca, where the bride had spent long childhood summers. They wanted a very Mediterranean wedding reflecting the beauty of the island.

Three events were held which sought to encompass "three Majorcas". On the first day there was a cocktail at the Hotel Formontor, in a magical cove. The decor sought to highlight the beauty of the area with warm lighting and flowers in wicker baskets and boxes for an informal feel. A singer entertained the audience with classic songs at the start of the evening, followed by a zappy DJ.

The religious ceremony was held in Muro, in the parish of San Juan Bautista. The guests then moved to Son Doblons, a nearby estate with views to the mountain and inland area full of orange trees and wonderful patios. For dinner, a large Mediterranean porch was recreated, with draped white linen curtains gathered back with bougainvillea twine to make it cozy. Candles hung from the trees to create a magical atmosphere.

The disco area had been divided into two spaces. In the first, outside, a live band kicked off the party among olive trees. Once this performance was over, the inside disco was discovered behind an enormous mirror, in a space decorated like a cave.

The next day was spent at the beach in Muro to enjoy the typical rice and fish at a beach bar. Flowers and personalized details predominated the decoration. The cocktail area was framed under a wall of bougainvillea in an orange grove. The tables were dressed with typical Majorcan ikat fabrics in blue and white decorated with Aloe Vera and *Echeveria*. The atmosphere was unbeatable: a perfect end to three amazing days.

The newlyweds, of Filipino and Italian origin, prepared some welcome packs with dried mango, limoncello, and a bowl of almonds, as well as the weekend program.

The Hotel Formentor's decor was intended to highlight the beauty of the area, with warm lighting and flowers in wicker baskets and boxes providing an informal feel to the event.

We endeavored to use seasonal flowers, such as hydrangeas, peonies, Lavender and Jasmine.

The lighting of the pine forest varied throughout the night: it began with a subtle ambient light and evolved towards different colors in motion, to provide depth and integrate the space in the dance area.

The bride's witnesses greeted the guests at the church entrance by distributing oriental-style fans for the heat and a souvenir of the event with a text written by the bride and groom.

The flower boys dressed casually with mandarin-collar shirts and green shorts matching the same-colored getup of the flower girls. As shoes, espadrilles for all.

The Church of St. John the
Baptist where the ceremony
was held is dominated by
an impressive Baroque
altarpiece.

At the end of the ceremony, the groom surprised the bride with a turquoise Fiat 500 that carried them to the celebration venue.

The main features of the decor were the flowers and all the personalized details. The cocktail area was framed under an impressive wall of bougainvillea in an orange grove.

The platters were painted especially
in the same line as the invitations
and the flowers on the tables.
With this special touch and green
glassware, flawless and, at the same
time, carefree tables were achieved.

For dinner, the intention was to
recreate a huge Mediterranean porch
with white linen curtains drawn
back with bougainvillea making a
cozy area. Flower arrangements also
hung from the balconies. The well,
that occupied the center space, was
also decorated so that everything was
brought together.

The disco area was divided into two spaces. In the first one, outside, a live band was in charge of entertaining the guests, who danced among the olive trees. The second one lay hidden behind a mirrored wall.

The bride danced with her father to the beat of *Good Vibrations,* by the Beach Boys to inaugurate the dance floor.

On the day at the beach, the
Ponderosa atmosphere prevailed,
with a festive and relaxed touch.
The tables were dressed with typical
Majorcan ikat fabrics in blue and
white, decorated with Aloe Vera and
Echeveria.

The columns were decorated
with bougainvillea and vines. The
atmosphere was unbeatable: a
perfect end to three amazing days.

A buffet with small tacos, snacks,
juices and rice impeccably presented.

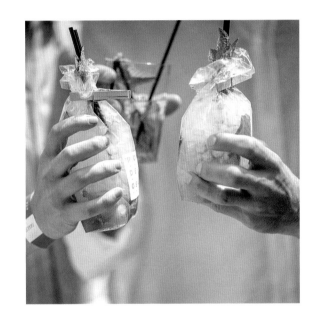

UNDER THE SUN
OF SOTOGRANDE

The wedding took place one August in Sotogrande. The bride and groom are polo and horse lovers and that's why they decided to celebrate the event on a polo field. They wanted their personality to be reflected without the wedding becoming just a horse theme. A Mediterranean summer wedding was devised using seasonal flowers and fruit: grapes, figs, pomegranates, dahlias, roses, hydrangeas, *Viburnum*... The idea was to find the balance between the sophistication of the flowers and the simplicity of the vases they were in.

When the guests were taken to the polo field, after the ceremony they found an impressive structure of greenery and flowers designed to close off the space and delimit the cocktail area. On each side of the structure, the guests encountered two transparent tents decorated with classical columns with wooden lamps on the ceiling to achieve a cozy dining area. The fact that there were two allowed a more familiar and relaxed atmosphere.

When dinner was over, the guests went to the disco, inspired by *The Great Gatsby*: all in black and gold with two backlit columns. The dance floor in the center of the tent was customized with the same motifs as the columns. A DJ had everyone dancing to his music until dawn.

The ceremony took place in the parish of Nuestra Señora de la Merced, where the kneeling benches were covered with typically Philippine pineapple fabric made to measure by the bride's mother.

The altar was decorated in green to cover the white background of the church. For the centerpieces green and white vases were chosen, very classical, with hydrangeas, suitably solemn for the ceremony.

In a polo field, a country wedding was designed with the sophisticated touch desired by the bride and groom and achieving the goal of bringing the field and the tents together with the help of the florists.

The cocktail area blended with the surrounding greenery thanks to structures lined with greens and bougainvillea.

Welcome packs in a wicker basket with almond and chocolate cookies and orange-blossom scented ceramic oranges a survival kit to celebrate the three-day wedding celebration and weekend program.

During the cocktail, the piano bar music greatly entertained the guests, who danced from then on.

Round tables alternating with tall and low centerpieces formed the dining area. The table cards depicted the same motif of palm leaves that could be seen all along the way to the wedding venue.

Dinner was served under transparent tents, which gave the feeling of being inside a sophisticated greenhouse.

The centerpieces with flowers and seasonal fruit: grapes, figs, pomegranates and pink dahlias and hydrangeas, to balance the sophistication of the flower and the simplicity of the vases and fruits.

A classic touch was provided
by columns, ceiling beams and
wooden chandeliers, produced
by A-tipica, which also served to
camouflage the structure of the
tent itself.

The disco, inspired by *The Great Gatsby*, was located between the two dining tents, at a lower level so as to allow watching and enjoying the dance scene from any angle.

THE SEVILLE BREEZE

Certain parties, the morning after, have already become legendary. That's the case of the wedding of a Norwegian-Arab couple, who decided to marry in Seville and contacted A-tipica recommended by an international wedding planner.

Respectful for the cultures of both bride and groom, the Andalusian roots served as a meeting point to inspire this marriage. On the first evening, the central courtyard of the emblematic Casa Guardiola—built in the nineteenth century—was filled with the aroma and view of orange groves, orange blossom and Mediterranean touches. An imposing buffet dinner with cocktails and show cooking was served at the tables arranged around the estate, wetting the guests' appetites for a party that culminated in Arabian dances until late night.

On the second day, the Molinillos ranch was dressed in a folkloric guise. So, the chords of the opera *Carmen*, the decoration reminiscent of the Sevillian Feria de Abril or the entrance to the villa, flanked by colorful baskets full of flowers and with an entourage of hostesses dressed in flamenco costumes, contrasted with the zenith and intimist lighting at the tables, enhancing their magnificent centerpieces. Inspired by Arabian tradition, the bride and groom entered the room to the rhythm of a melody from their native country, both melting into a dance that kicked off dinner. Divided into three courses at tables with carnations and fans, the evening was enlivened with flamenco performances and later on, a carnival atmosphere, in which the ladies could rest their feet at stands offering espadrilles and all the guests ended up surrendering to artisan churros.

Perhaps the most informal of nights, but the last night held many surprises. Jointly with the bride and groom, A-tipica found the Casa del Estanque, in the Maria Luisa Park, a dream stage for an incomparable party. A path of flowers made of fabric was arranged to guide the guests towards some lights with the words "Happily Ever After". In contrast to the austere and industrial furniture, the flowers became protagonists inside pineapples, coconuts or banana palm leaves. A cigar expert manufactured them on the spot, tailor-made for the guests who, while waiting, lingered among stalls offering lemonade, popcorn, cheese or handicrafts. A meeting point between the roots of two worlds was the reason for a magical weekend.

On the first evening, the central courtyard of the emblematic Casa Guardiola in Seville staged an unforgettable welcome cocktail.

Centerpieces with orange leaves and orange blossom were some of the Mediterranean touches that set the scene, which thanks to its Moorish architecture already provided a vintage and Andalusian touch.

A buffet-style dinner with show cooking in which the guests sat at different tables distributed around the courtyard.

The centerpieces were inspired by Andalusia and the Mediterranean. Importantly, the guests could try the walnuts, dates and other assorted nuts that had been placed inside the flowers and spread across the tables.

The cocktail consisted of a spectacular buffet of salads, typical Andalusian tapas and a grill with show cooking.

The main entertainment on the
first day was Arabian dances that
delighted the guests until well into
the night.

The second celebration day, the
wedding day, took place at the
Molinillos ranch located on the
outskirts of Seville. It was an evening
totally inspired by Andalusian
folklore with a touch of opera,
Carmen.

Castanets, fans and hostesses with flamenco costumes were chosen to highlight the most folkloric features of the event so the guests could really feel Seville upon arrival.

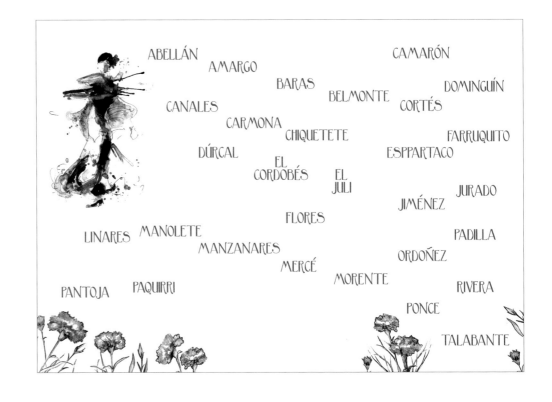

ABELLÁN   CAMARÓN
      AMARGO
         BARAS   DOMINGUÍN
               BELMONTE   CORTÉS
CANALES
    CARMONA
          CHIQUETETE   FARRUQUITO
DÚRCAL   ESPPARTACO
      EL
      CORDOBÉS   EL
              JULI   JURADO
                  JIMÉNEZ
        FLORES
LINARES   MANOLETE   PADILLA
      MANZANARES   ORDOÑEZ
         MERCÉ
           MORENTE
PANTOJA   PAQUIRRI   RIVERA
           PONCE
        TALABANTE

The entrance path to the ranch
was decorated with large baskets
of flowers in different colors.

For dinner in the courtyard, a very dim lighting was achieved thanks to tall bamboo poles, which helped to create the Zenithal lighting so common in A-tipica's staging, which highlights the centerpieces.

The centerpieces on the tables contained carnations, geraniums, roses, dahlias and chrysanthemums, and, along with candles, provided the tables with a lot of texture and color. Menu had been handwritten on fans to counter excessive heat, as well as being a very representative item of Spain.

The table place cards represented famous bull fighters and flamenco dancers, and had castanets attached, so the guests could use them throughout the evening joining in the fun.

Following the traditions of Arabian weddings, once the guests were seated and the dishes were served, the performances began. The attendees enjoyed different flamenco shows. The night went from dance to dance.

The Maria Luisa Park became a space full of color with gigantic hand-sewn flowers made by expert flamenco costume seamstresses, creating pathways full of light and color. At the end of the fabric flower trails, the phrase "Happily Ever After" shone in neon lights.

The space was decorated with somewhat industrial-looking furniture, the flowers were all from tropical fruits, such as pineapples, coconuts, banana palm leaves, etcetera. Different stalls were assembled: popcorn, lemonade, cheese and burgers.

Lia's services, rolling cigars on the spot, were hired, and an expert who arranged head scarves on the guests in the tropical style.

AN AUTUMN TALE

This wedding featured Carla, a partner at A-tipica, and her boyfriend Rafael, from Honduras. Therefore, being family, they trusted the company one hundred per cent, leaving A-tipica to choose the wedding venue and all the details. We decided it would be a fairytale wedding.

The concept of fairytale wedding began when the palace of Moratalla was found in Cordoba, restored and converted into a hotel a few months earlier. The creative freedom that this allowed and the novelty were key to its election. It was a perfect place to surprise all the guests, but especially foreign guests who were travelling to Europe for a wedding.

The large space pleaded for long imperial tables and this was the perfect choice to break away from the traditional round table, which was the usual thing at the time. The palace-like atmosphere marked the inspiration: To turn a garden into a classic interior hall with chandeliers and warm strong colors. The ceiling was formed by the treetops of the centennial trees on each side. All the graphics were completely customized, from the invitations to a logo with the initials of the bride and groom, embossed on the stationery, but also on ashtrays and linen napkins specially made for the day.

To decorate the two endless tables, movement was needed, so silver and glass tableware was mixed, many candles of varying heights and colors. In addition to flowers, fruits such as pomegranates, plums and grapes were used. It was the beginning of autumn and this should not go unnoticed. The tale ended with the performances of a big band and a DJ who delighted the Latino guests at a party as never before.

Aware of the palatial site where she would celebrate her wedding, Carla, from the A-tipica family, chose an elegant princess-style dress.

The ceremony was held in San Calixto, a cloistered convent. The chapel was very small which made the ceremony familiar and special.

The Palace of Moratalla, in Cordoba—with century-old trees, a garden of roses and boxwood mazes—was chosen to surprise the guests.

The guests moved in small trains from the palace entrance until the cocktail area.

The palatial setting influenced the inspiration: a classic Palace hall was created with chandeliers and warm colors, on an esplanade covered only by the treetops.

Setting up two tables—about seventy meters long each—to seat two hundred guests at each table, involved a great deal of logistics. The distance between areas, at the time of serving dinner, was a major concern, but, finally, it worked out fine, and all went smoothly.

The flowers in warm hues formed a range of oranges, reds, maroons, purples, in a variety of kinds, such as dahlias, roses of every variety, black calla lilies, and placed in different vases in order to decorate the two endless tables.

The graphics of the wedding were entirely customized. A logo was created with the bride's and groom's initials embossed on all the stationery, ashtrays and linen napkins made especially for the occasion.

Silver and glass tableware was mixed, as were the candles of different sizes and colors. In addition to flowers, fruits such as pomegranates, plums and grapes were used. The beginning of autumn should not go unnoticed.

The lighting was a warm and creative mixture. On the one hand, there were chandeliers and zenithal spotlights on the tables to highlight the centerpieces and, on the other, the trees were illuminated by a small green filter that brought magic to the setting and set off the colors.

NIGHT AMIDST TAPESTRIES

The Italian groom wanted to celebrate his wedding in Madrid, the City of the bride, and the couple needed to find an emblematic venue that would welcome guests from both countries attending their wedding. Therefore, when A-tipica proposed the Royal Tapestry Factory, they agreed this was the perfect place, also with the possibility of a small guided tour for the guests.

The civil ceremony was held in front of an impressive tapestry in one of the halls. Everything was staged in autumn colors using the lighting, crimson and green hues, and the reddish color of branches. Meanwhile, the exquisite notes of a string quartet could be heard.

The cocktail—entertained by a jazz trio—took place outdoors, in the small gardens with all the furniture supplied by A-tipica, suited to the setting. The guests then toured the tapestry halls while being given a brief explanation. The dinner was served in the Goya Hall, transformed into an autumn forest. The spot lighting focused on the center of the tables to highlight the flowers, candles, and an ambient indirect lighting in warm colors were essential to achieve the atmosphere of the season that marked the event.

The story of the wedding was that, despite being an Italian tradition that the bride and groom should cut the cake together, with the toast and speeches, during the pre-wedding menu tasting, Genoveva and Marco fell in love with the Arabian cake made of wafers and cream, so a mirror structure was devised to emulate a multi-layered cake. They only cut the top one. The party ended with the performance of a DJ, who dazzled with music and lighting tricks suited to this celebration.

The Royal Tapestry Factory of Madrid was the emblematic venue that hosted the couple and their guests on their wedding day. The civil ceremony took place in one of its halls beneath an impressive tapestry. The seating plan was one of the most carefully supervised details of the wedding. As the groom is a photographer, they used pictures taken by him, writing the names of the guests on them.

The atmosphere, achieved with
flowers, was inspired by the colors
of autumn, season during which
the wedding was celebrated, while
maintaining the solemn aura of the
setting. Green and reddish hues were
used.

Crema de Boletus

Lomos de Lubina al aroma de trufa
y almendras con salsa de cava

Magret de pato con salsa de arándanos
acompañado de Patatitas doradas
con mantequilla y perejil
y
Bastoncitos de verduras al dente

Tarta árabe de obleas fritas
con almendras caramelizadas

Marques de Riscal Rueda verdejo

Azpilicueta Rioja Reserva 2009

Montesquius Brut Reserva

Veva & Marco
Madrid, 17 de Octubre de 2015

The dinner was served in the Goya
Hall, transformed by A-tipica into an
autumn forest.

Spotlights focused on the center
of the tables to highlight the
centerpieces of flowers. In addition,
an indirect ambient light in warm
colors and hundreds of candles,
spread around the hall, played a
key role in achieving the desired
autumnal warmth.

The tapestries hanging in the hall
were spotlit and given a major role
placing bouquets in greens and
candles at the same height. Things
blended into each other superbly.

A mirror structure was created with
the wafer cakes emulating a huge
bridal cake. The bride and groom
cut the top layer and divided the rest
among all the guests.

ALL I WANT
FOR CHRISTMAS IS YOU

When Christmas weddings were still not a very widespread custom in Spain, Mariate and Alfonso came to A-tipica ready to be married in December in Cartagena (Murcia) in a pine forest belonging to a family quarry. The season and the closeness of Christmas became the main inspiration for a wedding in which red hues, fireplaces, pine cones and olive trees took the leading role. The bride decorated the church in an especially Christmassy style, with all the flowers in shades of green and red.

The guests were greeted with a message at the entrance, "All I Want for Christmas is You", which reflected the spirit of greetings and celebration. Along the entrance path, still lifes with pine cones, pomegranates, eucalyptus and glass bottles predicted the celebration to be held.

The cocktails were held outside with braziers for warmth and a Christmas atmosphere and the lunch was served in small burgundy-colored tents. Great care was taken with the table design where the flower centerpieces had a Christmas touch in white and green, and cotton-plant flowers emulated snow in golden vases. As napkin holder, Christmas tree decorations were used, such as wooden reindeer and stars.

Tartan fabrics, a sky of cotton flowers or a Christmas tree where guests could leave their messages, were just some of the touches that wrapped the wedding in a Christmas spirit, a wedding to always be remembered as one of the best.

The bride displayed a spectacular embroidery design on the back of her dress.

The bridal bouquet,
with velvety red roses
and eucalyptus, was
in keeping with the
inspiration of the
wedding.

At the entrance to the groom's family estate, the phrase "All I Want for Christmas is You" was painted on the wall to greet guests.

MARIATE
Y
ALFONSO

HUERTO DE SAN PEDRO

Along the entrance way, the guests encountered still lifes with pine cones, olive trees, eucalyptus and glass bottles.

The lunch was served inside
tents. The tables were carefully
decorated with Christmas
centerpieces of flowers in white,
green and with cotton flowers in
golden vases.

The numbers of the tables were
golden blocks, the glassware was
plum-colored and Christmas tree
decorations, such as wooden reindeer
and stars, were used as napkin
holders.

The sun allowed for cocktails outdoors with the help of braziers to warm up and bonfires made to measure which were very decorative, as well as practical.

As an after-hours snack, chestnuts were roasted on the fire. An original option that added atmosphere to this winter wedding.

The cotton plants were certainly the magic touch of the event. Thousands of branches of this plant covered the ceiling simulating snow.

On the giant Christmas tree
the guests found the message
"Leave a memory on the tree,"
which encouraged them to share
their best wishes with the bride
and groom.

GRACIAS
POR VENIR!

DEJA TU
RECUERDO
EN EL ÁRBOL

EDITED BY
A-TIPICA
www.a-tipica.com

TEXTS
Cristina Ruiz Montesinos

TRANSLATION
Art in Translation

PRODUCTION
Ediciones El Viso

DESIGN
Subiela Bernat

PHOTO CREDITS
Click 10: pp. 30–39
Bibiana Fierro: pp. 106–17
Mora Figueroa: pp. 154–75
Victoria Muñoz: p. 14
Patricia Salinero and Click 10: p. 15
Javier Sancho: pp. 4, 11, 12, 18–29,
40–87, 190–215
Javier Sancho and Bibiana Fierro:
pp. 10, 88–105
Javier Sancho and Click 10: pp. 6–7,
118–39
Javier Sancho, Liven Photography,
and Render Emotion: pp. 140–53
Javier Sancho and Montelena:
pp. 176–89
Javier Sancho and Victoria Muñoz:
pp. 14–17

PREPRESS
Emilio Breton

TYPESETTING
Nicolás García Marque

PRINTING
Brizzolis

BINDING
Ramos

ISBN: 978-84-947466-1-1
DL: M-29463-2017
Printed in Spain

Ediciones El Viso
128 Castelló, 28006 Madrid
+ 34 91 519 65 76
www.edicioneselviso.com